Spelling Today

for ages 7-8

...includes words, spelling patterns and
spelling rules recommended for
Year 3 pupils.

How to use this book:

1. Look at the rules and words featured on the right-hand pages.

2. Turn over the page to look at each word on the left-hand page.

3. Cover the word with the flap, then write the word.

4. Uncover the word to check that you haven't made a mistake.

5. Write the word again for extra practice.

Adding ing (1)

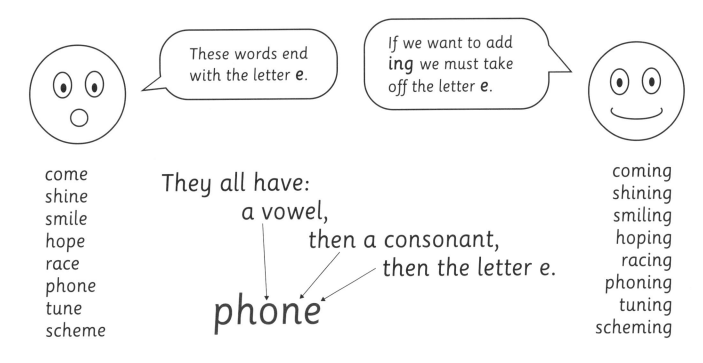

These words end with the letter **e**.

If we want to add **ing** we must take off the letter **e**.

come
shine
smile
hope
race
phone
tune
scheme

They all have:
a vowel,
then a consonant,
then the letter e.

phone

coming
shining
smiling
hoping
racing
phoning
tuning
scheming

Fill in the missing words, using the ing words above.

Are you _____ home today?

When Anne and Peter were _____ with each other, Peter tripped over.

The piano tuner is _____ the old piano.

They were _____ that the sun would be _____ .

Mum is _____ the doctor.

Nick and Richard are _____ because they are _____

together to trick the teacher.

3

Step 1	Step 2	Step 3
Look and learn, then cover the word with the flap.	Write the word then see if it's correct.	Write the word again. Say it as you write it.
come		
coming		
shine		
shining		
smile		
smiling		
hope		
hoping		
race		
racing		
phone		
phoning		
tune		
tuning		
scheme		
scheming		

4

Adding ing (3)

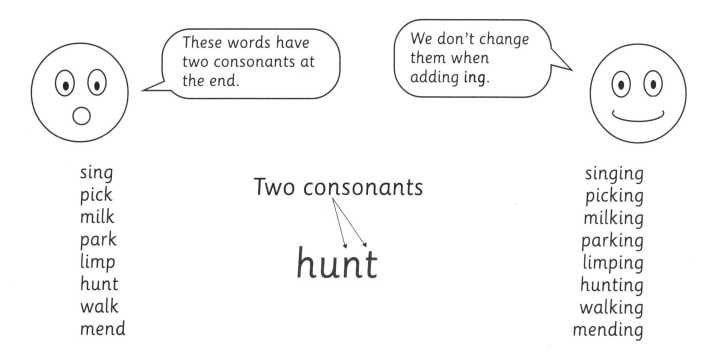

These words have two consonants at the end.

We don't change them when adding ing.

sing	singing
pick	picking
milk	milking
park	parking
limp	limping
hunt	hunting
walk	walking
mend	mending

Two consonants

hunt

Fill in the missing words, using the **ing** words above.

Alex was _____ loudly while _____ the cows.

Lizzie is _____ up litter from the car _____ spaces.

Jasdeep was _____ along quite normally, then she suddenly

started _____ .

I'll be _____ the broken washing machine tomorrow.

Chris was _____ for the pencil he lost.

7

Step 1 Look and learn, then cover the word with the flap.	Step 2 Write the word then see if it's correct.	Step 3 Write the word again. Say it as you write it.
sing		
singing		
pick		
picking		
milk		
milking		
park		
parking		
limp		
limping		
hunt		
hunting		
walk		
walking		
mend		
mending		

Adding ing (4)

These words have two vowels before the final consonant.

We don't change them when we add ing.

clean		cleaning
dream		dreaming
sleep	Two vowels	sleeping
shoot		shooting
boil	shout	boiling
nail		nailing
haul		hauling
shout		shouting

There are eight more words to add **ing** to:

sweep ⟶

sail ⟶

float ⟶

rain ⟶

aim ⟶

eat ⟶

join ⟶

look ⟶

Step 1	Step 2	Step 3
Look and learn, then cover the word with the flap.	Write the word then see if it's correct.	Write the word again. Say it as you write it.
cleaning		
dreaming		
sleeping		
shooting		
boiling		
nailing		
hauling		
shouting		
sweeping		
sailing		
floating		
raining		
aiming		
eating		
joining		
looking		

Words with le

Words which end with le...

...sometimes have double consonants in the middle.

Here are some words with double letters:

paddle   kettle   giggle   wobble   middle

Can you think of some double letter words which end in le?

Try to think of an extra le word for each of these sets:

table vegetable	bicycle circle	needle bundle	prickle chuckle

double grumble	terrible possible	crumple example

Step 1 Look and learn, then cover the word with the flap.	Step 2 Write the word then see if it's correct.	Step 3 Write the word again. Say it as you write it.
saddle		
kettle		
little		
middle		
nozzle		
bottle		
puddle		
bubble		
cable		
uncle		
tickle		
candle		
trouble		
horrible		
simple		
handle		

Prefixes

We can change the meaning of some words...

...just by putting a prefix at the start.

Look: 'Is your room tidy?'
        'No, it's untidy.'

Practise these words		Add the prefix to the word			Write the new word
usual		un	+	usual	
lucky		un	+	lucky	
code		de	+	code	
like		dis	+	like	
appear		dis	+	appear	
agree		dis	+	agree	
cycle		re	+	cycle	
play		re	+	play	
trained		un	+	trained	
qualify		dis	+	qualify	
fix		pre	+	fix	
write		re	+	write	
sense		non	+	sense	
possible		im	+	possible	
visible		in	+	visible	
clockwise		anti	+	clockwise	

Step 1	Step 2	Step 3
Look and learn, then cover the word with the flap.	Write the word then see if it's correct.	Write the word again. Say it as you write it.
lucky		
unlucky		
usual		
unusual		
appear		
disappear		
agree		
disagree		
cycle		
recycle		
write		
rewrite		
sense		
nonsense		
possible		
impossible		

Suffixes

We can change the meaning of some words...

...just by putting a suffix at the end.

Look: My dad is tall,

but my mum is tall**er**.

My gran is tall**est** of all.

Fill in the gaps.

Word	+ er	+ est
cold	colder	
long		
dark		
light		

Look what happens to words which end with e:

late   later   latest

Word	+ er	+ est
fine	finer	
nice		
rude		
	closer	

Step 1	Step 2	Step 3
Look and learn, then cover the word with the flap.	Write the word then see if it's correct.	Write the word again. Say it as you write it.
dark		
darker		
darkest		
light		
lighter		
lightest		
coldest		
nicer		
finest		
rude		
rudest		
close		
closer		
closest		
tall		
taller		

More suffixes

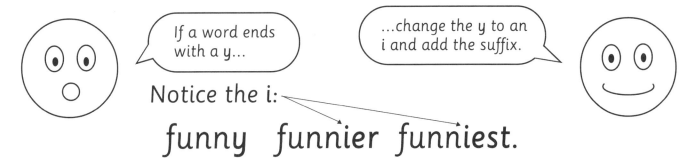

If a word ends with a y...

...change the y to an i and add the suffix.

Notice the i:

funny   funnier   funniest.

Fill in the gaps:

Word	+ er	+ est
funny	funnier	
runny		
happy		
lucky		

If words have a short vowel, then a consonant at the end...

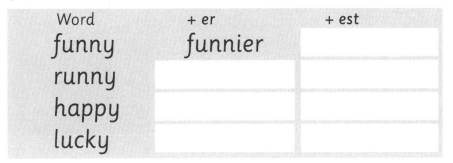

sad   sadder   saddest

...double the consonant.

Word	+ er	+ est
big	bigger	
fit		
hot		
	wetter	

Step 1	Step 2	Step 3
Look and learn, then cover the word with the flap.	Write the word then see if it's correct.	Write the word again. Say it as you write it.
funny		
funnier		
funniest		
happy		
happier		
happiest		
lucky		
luckiest		
bigger		
biggest		
thin		
thinner		
thinnest		
hotter		
hottest		
wettest		

18

Even more suffixes

Is the sun out today?

Yes, it's very sunny.

Look at the word:

one short vowel
↓
s**u**n
↑
one consonant

To add the suffix y:

su**nn**y
↑ ↑
...we double the consonant.

These words work the same way:

run	→		fun	→	
nip	→		nut	→	

Just add y to these words:

crisp	→	crispy	cheek	→	
frill	→		fizz	→	

Take the **e** off these words:

shine	→	shiny	stone	→	
smoke	→		rose	→	

Step 1	Step 2	Step 3
Look and learn, then cover the word with the flap.	Write the word then see if it's correct.	Write the word again. Say it as you write it.
runny		
nutty		
crispy		
cheeky		
frilly		
fizzy		
shiny		
rosy		
stony		
water		
smoky		
watery		
fur		
furry		
grease		
greasy		

Singular and Plural

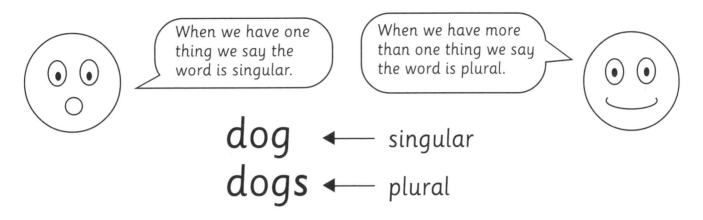

When we have one thing we say the word is singular.

When we have more than one thing we say the word is plural.

dog ← singular
dogs ← plural

Here are some ways to make singular words become plural:

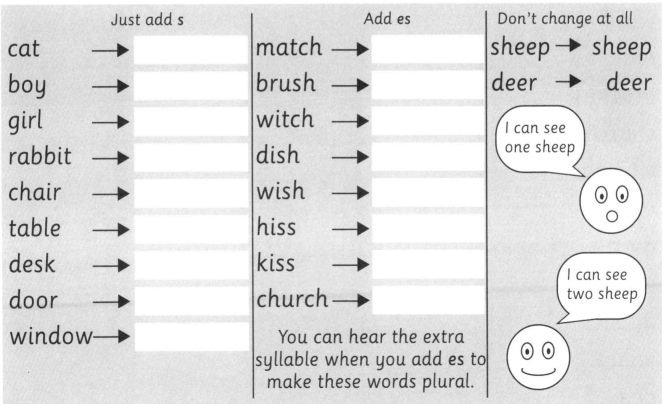

Just add s	Add es	Don't change at all
cat →	match →	sheep → sheep
boy →	brush →	deer → deer
girl →	witch →	
rabbit →	dish →	I can see one sheep
chair →	wish →	
table →	hiss →	
desk →	kiss →	
door →	church →	I can see two sheep
window →		

You can hear the extra syllable when you add es to make these words plural.

21

Step 1	Step 2	Step 3
Look and learn, then cover the word with the flap.	Write the word then see if it's correct.	Write the word again. Say it as you write it.
rabbits		
chairs		
tables		
desks		
doors		
windows		
matches		
brushes		
churches		
wishes		
boys		
girls		
witches		
ditches		
kisses		
deer		

More plurals

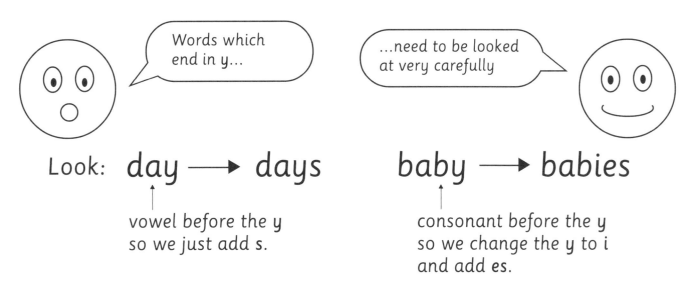

Words which end in y...

...need to be looked at very carefully

Look: day → days

vowel before the y so we just add **s**.

baby → babies

consonant before the y so we change the y to i and add **es**.

Follow the y rules to make these words plural:

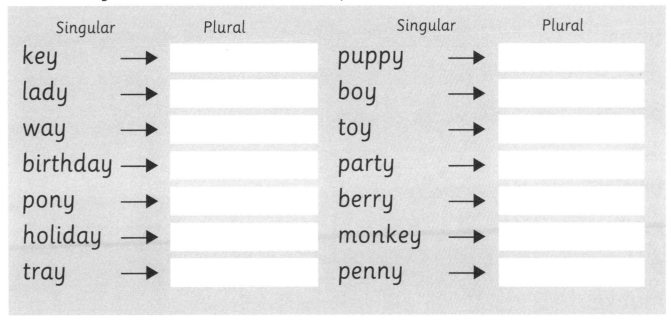

Singular	Plural	Singular	Plural
key →		puppy →	
lady →		boy →	
way →		toy →	
birthday →		party →	
pony →		berry →	
holiday →		monkey →	
tray →		penny →	

Step 1	Step 2	Step 3
Look and learn, then cover the word with the flap.	Write the word then see if it's correct.	Write the word again. Say it as you write it.
lady		
ladies		
birthday		
birthdays		
holiday		
holidays		
tray		
trays		
pony		
ponies		
baby		
babies		
party		
parties		
monkey		
monkeys		

24

Strange plurals

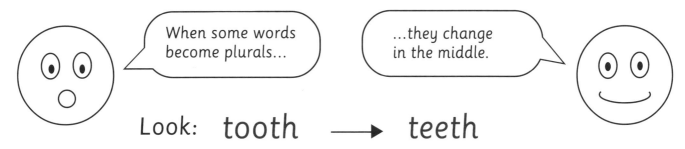

When some words become plurals...

...they change in the middle.

Look: tooth ⟶ teeth

Some words have a different ending when they become plurals.

Look: child ⟶ children

Find words in the word-bank to fill the gaps :

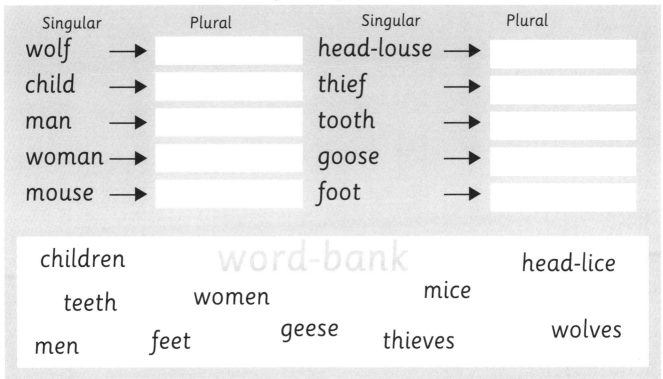

Singular	Plural	Singular	Plural
wolf ⟶		head-louse ⟶	
child ⟶		thief ⟶	
man ⟶		tooth ⟶	
woman ⟶		goose ⟶	
mouse ⟶		foot ⟶	

word-bank

children   head-lice

teeth   women   mice

men   feet   geese   thieves   wolves

Step 1	Step 2	Step 3
Look and learn, then cover the word with the flap.	Write the word then see if it's correct.	Write the word again. Say it as you write it.
child		
children		
thief		
thieves		
goose		
geese		
woman		
women		
mouse		
mice		
tooth		
teeth		
wolf		
wolves		
head-louse		
head-lice		

Silent letters

Some words have silent letters...

...which can make the words hard to spell.

Silent b words

comb

bomb

crumb

lamb

thumb

Silent g words

gnat

gnome

gnaw

gnash

Silent h words

when

where

why

chemist

rhyme

what

Silent k words

knee

knife

knight

knock

know

knuckle

Silent l words

could

would

should

calf

half

chalk

calm

palm

Silent w words

wreck

write

wrist

wrap

wrong

answer

sword

wrapping

Step 1	Step 2	Step 3
Look and learn, then cover the word with the flap.	Write the word then see if it's correct.	Write the word again. Say it as you write it.
lamb		
thumb		
half		
could		
would		
should		
rhyme		
write		
answer		
wrap		
wrong		
gnat		
knee		
knife		
know		
knight		

Adding ful and less

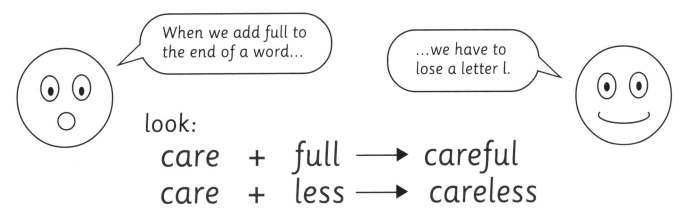

When we add full to the end of a word...

...we have to lose a letter l.

look:
care + full ⟶ careful
care + less ⟶ careless

Fill in the missing words:

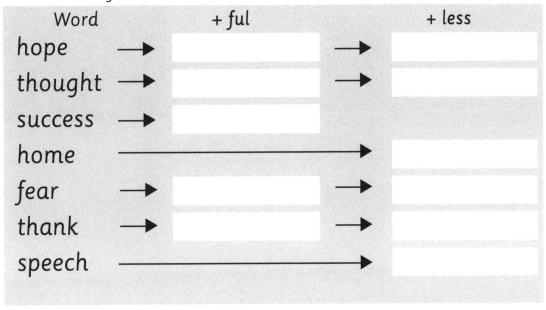

Word	+ ful	+ less
hope ⟶		
thought ⟶		
success ⟶		
home		
fear ⟶		
thank ⟶		
speech		

look:
beauty ⟶ beautiful

Step 1	Step 2	Step 3
Look and learn, then cover the word with the flap.	Write the word then see if it's correct.	Write the word again. Say it as you write it.
careful		
careless		
beauty		
beautiful		
hope		
hopeful		
hopeless		
thought		
thoughtful		
thoughtless		
speech		
speechless		
thank		
thankful		
fear		
fearful		

30

Compound words

Sometimes we make new words...

...by joining others together.

Fill in the gaps below:

some + times →	
some + thing →	
some + body →	
some + where →	
every + thing →	
every + body →	
every + where →	
no + thing →	
no + body →	
no + where →	
any + thing →	
any + body →	
any + where →	

sun + shine →	
play + time →	
play + ground →	
day + light →	
ever + green →	
ever + lasting →	
foot + ball →	
basket + ball →	
goal + keeper →	
week + end →	
motor + way →	
dust + bin →	
sea + side →	
sand + castle →	

Step 1	Step 2	Step 3
Look and learn, then cover the word with the flap.	Write the word then see if it's correct.	Write the word again. Say it as you write it.
somewhere		
everywhere		
nowhere		
anywhere		
somebody		
everybody		
something		
everything		
anything		
seaside		
sunshine		
sandcastle		
football		
basketball		
weekend		
playground		

Using apostrophes

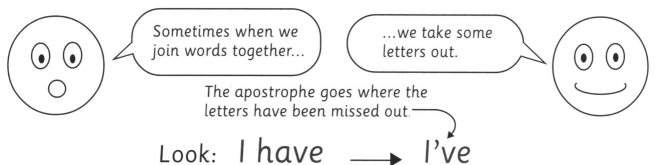

Sometimes when we join words together...

...we take some letters out.

The apostrophe goes where the letters have been missed out.

Look: I have ⟶ I've

Find words in the word-bank to fill the gaps :

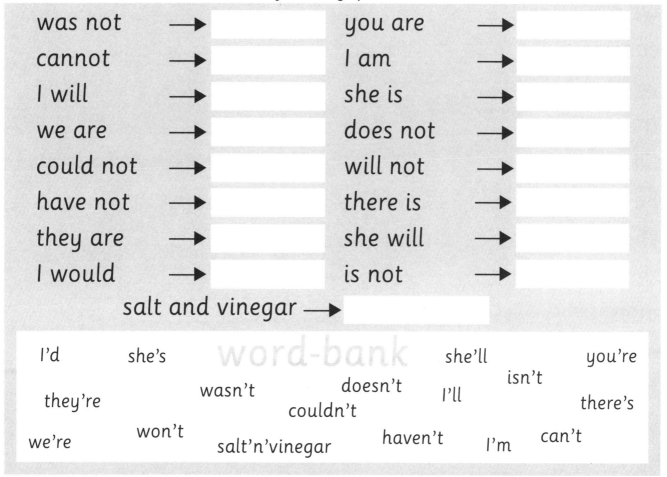

was not	⟶		you are	⟶
cannot	⟶		I am	⟶
I will	⟶		she is	⟶
we are	⟶		does not	⟶
could not	⟶		will not	⟶
have not	⟶		there is	⟶
they are	⟶		she will	⟶
I would	⟶		is not	⟶

salt and vinegar ⟶

word-bank

I'd   she's   she'll   you're

they're   wasn't   doesn't   I'll   isn't   there's
                    couldn't

we're   won't   salt'n'vinegar   haven't   I'm   can't

33

Step 1	Step 2	Step 3
Look and learn, then cover the word with the flap.	Write the word then see if it's correct.	Write the word again. Say it as you write it.
wasn't		
couldn't		
you're		
we're		
can't		
won't		
they're		
I'll		
he'll		
she'll		
there's		
does		
doesn't		
haven't		
wouldn't		
shouldn't		

34

Names and addresses

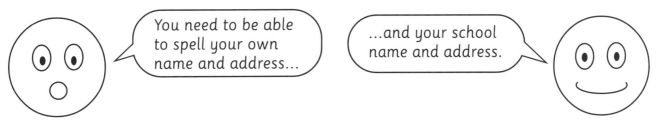

You need to be able to spell your own name and address...

...and your school name and address.

Ask an adult to help you to fill these addresses in:

Full name:

Address:

Postcode:

School name:

Address:

Postcode:

Step 1 Look and learn, then cover the word with the flap.	Step 2 Write the word then see if it's correct.	Step 3 Write the word again. Say it as you write it.
letter		
envelope		
address		
school		
postcode		
telephone		
post office		
Royal		
Mail		
stamp		
computer		
internet		
e-mail		
fax		
postcard		
parcel		